On The Right Track

*A Mini Wisdom Guide For Aligning
With Right Opportunities
That Honor Your Worth*

Alicia "WATERS"

**Foreword By:
Joseph L. Jones Jr.**

Copyright © 2014 Alicia "WATERS"

All rights reserved. Except for use in the case of brief quotations embodied in critical articles and reviews, the reproduction or utilization of this work in whole or part in any form by any electronic, digital, mechanical or other means, now known or hereafter invented, including xerography, photocopying, scanning, recording, or any information storage or retrieval system, is forbidden without prior written permission of the author and publisher.

The scanning, uploading, and distribution of this book via the Internet or via any other means without permission of the publisher and author is illegal and punishable by law. Purchase only authorized versions of this book and do not participate in or encourage electronic piracy of copyrighted materials. Your support of the author's rights is appreciated. Names, characters, places, and incidents are based on the author's own personal experience therefore names of persons and entities remain unnamed to protect the integrity of the story and the privacy of those involved. Any group or organization listed is for informational purposes only and does not imply endorsement or support of their activities or organization.

For ordering, booking, permission, or questions, contact the author.
www.anwempires@gmail.com

ISBN-13:978-1495952036

Printed in the United States of America by Create Space

On The Right Track

Dedication & Acknowledgments

This is a general dedication to everyone who is consciously aligning themselves to get on, be on and stay on the right track towards their holistic success.

I would like to give thanks to God and to all who have assisted me with guidance to be on the right track. I would like to acknowledge those who have allowed and entrusted me with helping them get on their right tracks to fulfill their purpose.

Special thanks to Joseph L. Jones Jr. for his wonderful contribution of an amazing foreword to this work.

On The Right Track

Table Of Contents

Foreword: On The Right Track

Introduction

Which Right Is Right At The Right Time?

Partnering With Your Bank Account

Choose Only Worthwhile Collateral Opportunities

Does Your Bank Account Have Wings?

Calculate Before Conception: Is This Wealth Creation Endeavor Worth It?

Which Opportunity Is Top Priority? Go For The Golden One

Having A Now & Later Plan Goes A Long Way

Listen To Your Inner Money Wisdom

Being Rightly Seen

Conclusion

On The Right Track

Foreword:
On The Right Track

Our ability to determine the most feasible route to our destination is imperative. In life, we are presented with many different tracks to take. Venturing down a poorly aligned path can prove to be catastrophic.

Building our future on the right track is an essential component to the prosperous advancement of our lives. We are gifted to receive this insight on this subject from Alicia "WATERS". She does a terrific job of encouraging us to take a deeper look at the decisions we make to build our future.

This writing sets us out on a journey to our desired future self by establishing the groundwork for us to arrive securely in Spirit, mind, and resources. The tracks of our lives are determined by our mindset. This book gives up important points of consideration.

We are worthy of the very best results. It is up to us to align and establish our right track for success. This powerful mini-book, crammed with useful tips, will help ensure that less time is wasted backtracking through life.

                    The Owner of Moundbuilders Inc.
                          ~Joseph L. Jones Jr.

On The Right Track

Introduction

There are three key areas where individuals often sell themselves short. The areas of time, value and money. Often, this primarily occurs in the areas of relationships, professions, and recreation.

Those three significant areas are often abused, neglected or mismanaged. Mainly in the world of business, especially in solo-entrepreneurship, coaches, consultants or practitioners often trade dollars for hours. In turn, this results in a lack of effectiveness for leveraging time, value and money.

Time, value and money are areas that truly deserve to be respected and honored especially if we desire to see more abundance flow into our lives. Often, when any of these areas are abused as it relates to the work that we do, the question of worthiness needs to be addressed.

Examining your worth concerning every area of life is critical. Doing an honest inventory to assess how we are respecting time, value and money will provide us with a measurable tracking system of our worthiness.

If we desire to see greater manifestations flow into our lives, then we must begin to honor and value ourselves with time and money. It's time to stop selling ourselves short so that we can attract that which we desire.

On The Right Track

Which Right Is Right At The Right Time?

I came across a question once on the facebook fan page of million dollar marketing coach, Kendall Summerhawk, where she asked the question; Are you more worried about doing things right, or doing the right things?

This is a question I ask myself often, in fact almost every other day when it comes to my personal affairs and especially as it relates to making business decisions. Trying to figure out which right is right can be a bit challenging at times.

I believe that there is a divine balance in having the ability to operate from both ends of the coin when necessary. The catch is trying to figure out which right is right at the right time. In the children's show Barney, there is a character named Baby Bop who sang a song once called, What should I do? When I don't know what I should do?

So what should you do? Which right is right? I've chosen to adopt a no "Wrong Way" approach by choosing what I believe that love would do in my current situations. This invites me to move out of stagnation, make my decisions right for me. There is no wrong way because love always chooses right.

On The Right Track

Partnering With Your Bank Account

Every day is a perfect day to partner with your bank account. This begins with making a new vow to yourself about honoring your worth by choosing to only engage in divine right inspired actions. Choose endeavors that are going to allow you to make the most of your time, earn what you deserve and invest wisely.

Partner with your bank account in the present by making a commitment that you will fill your bank account with worthwhile collateral. No more trading dollars for hours or giving away too much for too little. Your bank account is your intuitive partner who is ready to co-create the financial status that you desire.

Choose Only Worthwhile Collateral Opportunities

I'm sure most have seen the commercial for the Klondike Bar, where they ask the question; What would you do for a Klondike Bar? Sometimes we have to ask ourselves what would we do to truly be financially successful.

This challenge is a true test of character and our resolve to see if we will sell our souls through blood sweat and tears to make a dollar or will we find ways to create income by not settling for less.

I have a concept that I call, worthwhile collateral. This is where I challenge myself to only do work that is going to be worthwhile and lucrative. I've made a vow to myself to commit to truly honoring my worth on all levels. Therefore, I carefully examine how I'm going to spend my time as it relates to making money.

On The Right Track

If it's not worthwhile, I won't even entertain it. By getting clear, the universe can help to do the research and orchestrate opportunities for you to embark upon.

Only choosing worthwhile collateral is not just about choosing great money making opportunities, it's about engaging in a holistic total well-being framework that will yield prosperous short and long-term success.

Does Your Bank Account Have Wings?

Are your financial desires or goals bringing you wings yet? Lamarck and his "wishing" theory stills hold true. He claimed that birds do not fly because they have wings, but they have wings because they wanted to fly. We need to ask ourselves regularly; Does my bank account have wings yet?

Every day we need to examine our activities to evaluate whether or not our efforts will help us to accomplish our short to long-term goals. We should have quality goals that are soaring on opulent levels and bringing us the rewards of an abundant harvest.

It's time to take inventory of your profit strategies, along with mastering your inner game to see if you have truly partnered with your bank account in order for your efforts to deliver the results that you desire.

On The Right Track

Calculate Before Conception:
Is This Wealth Creation Endeavor Worth It?

Wise wealth building principles often consist of strategic intuitively aligned planning towards your financial goals. I've developed a concept called "Calculate Before Conception."

Before embarking on certain opportunities that could potentially increase my income, I ask myself, is this wealth opportunity worth it?

Several of us have had the experiences of jumping in to get rich quick scams or operations that desire for you to invest money up front in order to build a business under their umbrella only to find out that it wasn't what you thought.

Wise wealth building takes time, focus and goal setting to achieve the long-term results that are worth it. Calculate the opportunities that present themselves before beginning the co-creative efforts of engaging in something that is simply not worth it in the long run.

These are some of the thoughts that we should begin to entertain before quote on quote jumping into bed with a low-end opportunity.

Which Opportunity Is Top Priority?

On The Right Track

Go For The Golden One

There is an old saying that everything that glitters isn't gold. This implies that every shining golden opportunity that presents itself isn't always what it's cracked up to be. However, I believe that there are times when you have to have what I call the Olympic moment. Going for the gold is the only mentality that you can have on your way to achieving your highest levels of success in that arena.

The time is now for living our best life ever, a golden lifestyle. There are several opportunities that present themselves for us to act on, however, we must carefully evaluate those endeavors and make sure that we are on the right track.

Having A Now & Later Plan Goes A Long Way

I believe in having a now and later plan for almost everything. I know that you can't necessarily always plan one for everything, however, when it comes to leveraging time and creating lasting wealth, having a now and later plan goes a long way.

Having a now and later plan allows you to play on both sides of the track while continuing to move forward. Like the candy, Now & Later, you get to savor the moment while working in the present along with being at ease knowing that you have a follow-up system in place for advancement to support your efforts.

On The Right Track

But you have to begin taking action in the "Now" on your goals and not choose to put things off until later. Having a "Now & Later," plan is like having insurance, if you should run into a situation that stalls you on your forward movement, then you might be able to bring forth some of your pre-planning insights from your later agenda to support you in the present.

Listen To Your Inner Money Wisdom

Decide to take some time out to listen to your inner money wisdom to gain clarity before moving forward with your wealth creation goals. In order to be in full alignment with your money path remember to always make sure that you're feeding the right piggy bank opportunities.

Like partnering with your bank account, connecting with your inner money wisdom intuitively allows you to hear what the energy of money is speaking about on a higher level. This wisdom can help to launch you into the next realm of success that is more than you can imagine.

Slowing down, doing some deep breathing and tuning out all of the noise and information overload can assist you with opening up to a wealth creation idea that you would not have considered. Again, your inner money wisdom can reveal to you a higher perspective about a current idea that you're working on.

On The Right Track

Being Rightly Seen

There was a time when I was very concerned about not being seen or having enough visibility on certain social media platforms as it related to being known as a brand in my business.

At times I felt like I was invisible and no matter how much talent I had, there just seem to be no real interest in who I was or what my services had to offer.

After doing several years of inner game work, I began to focus on seeing myself clearly first and not focusing so much on whether I was being seen or not.

I learned to become visible to myself. I once heard the visionary and intuitive coach, Anya Sophia Mann say; "that we do not need anyone to see us in order to be seen. We do not need anyone to hear us in order to be heard. We do not need anyone to feel us in order for us to feel ourselves."

I've come to realize that it's not about having so many people to see you that counts. It's about rightly being seen by yourself and the right people who need to see you at the right time.

George Bernard Shaw, says; *"Better see rightly on a pound a week than squint on a million."*

Antoine de Saint-Exupery, says; *"It's is only with the heart that one can see rightly; what is essential is invisible to the eye."*

On The Right Track

Both of those statements correctly express how wisdom combined with the passion that flows from your heart space is what aligns your inner sight to rightly see what your soul desires to express. This will eventually reflect in the outward manifestations towards your visibility.

Sometimes not being seen by others might be serving you. Again, you want to be seen by the right people at the right time. As mentioned earlier, the focus in the present should be kept on rightly seeing yourself the way that Source sees you.

On The Right Track

Conclusion

Often we question our true worth and what truly makes us valuable. Before we can truly come to understand the depths of that question, we need to understand what our true value is not.

Our true value is not in the amount of money that we have, the number of people who approve of us or in the illusion of being in a certain economic class. Nor is our value determined by our history or past failures or successes. Though we can learn from our history and our experiences from the past, we must understand that our value lies in the present moment of our "Now Potential."

We each have value to add and to gain in the "Now." There are unlimited possibilities that are waiting for us to explore. We will begin to experience new levels of our worth when we tap into our greater potential and share it with the world at large.

It's time to truly value ourselves, get out of the past or eliminate whatever is holding us back and realize that our value lies in our "Now Potential."

On The Right Track

On The Right Track
Planner & Action Section

On The Right Track

On The Right Track Action Planning

Record your insights from the reading and create an action plan in the planning guide.

Questions & Thoughts To Consider:

I feel on track when I'm...

I'm wondering what would help me stay on track?

What is mine to do right now?

I'm curious to know or learn...

Actions To Consider

Write a daily, weekly or monthly action plan to keep moving forward on the right track.

Decide how you are going to execute your goals.

Celebrate along the way for every completed task big or small.

On The Right Track

On The Right Track Action Planning

On The Right Track

Continued Planning:

On The Right Track

On The Right Track Action Planning

On The Right Track

Continued Planning:

On The Right Track

On The Right Track Action Planning

On The Right Track

Continued Planning:

On The Right Track

On The Right Track Action Planning

On The Right Track

Continued Planning:

On The Right Track

On The Right Track Action Planning

On The Right Track

Continued Planning:

On The Right Track

On The Right Track Action Planning

On The Right Track

Continued Planning:

On The Right Track

On The Right Track Action Planning

On The Right Track

Continued Planning:

On The Right Track

On The Right Track Action Planning

On The Right Track

Continued Planning:

On The Right Track

On The Right Track Action Planning

On The Right Track

Continued Planning:

On The Right Track

On The Right Track Action Planning

On The Right Track

Continued Planning:

On The Right Track

On The Right Track Action Planning

On The Right Track

Continued Planning:

On The Right Track

On The Right Track Action Planning

On The Right Track

Continued Planning:

On The Right Track

On The Right Track Action Planning

Continued Planning:

On The Right Track

On The Right Track Action Planning

On The Right Track

Continued Planning:

On The Right Track

For More Resources

Visit:
www.amazon.com/author/alicianwaters

Or

To Book The Author For Speaking Engagements

Email: www.anwempires@gmail.com

If you enjoyed this resource, please consider writing a review on Amazon.com .

Thanks & Blessings

On The Right Track

www.ingramcontent.com/pod-product-compliance
Lightning Source LLC
Chambersburg PA
CBHW071828170526
45167CB00003B/1467